REFORMING ASIA'S LARGEST PRISON COMPLEX

TRANSFORMING PRISONS

Dr. Kiran Bedi

DIAMOND BOOKS

www.diamondbooks.in

Publisher : **Diamond Pocket Books (P) Ltd.**
X-30, Okhla Industrial Area,
Phase-II, New Delhi-110020
Phone : 011-40712200
E-mail : wecare@diamondbooks.in
Website : www.diamondbooks.in
Edition : 2025

TRANSFORMING PRISONS
Author - Dr. Kiran Bedi

Author's Note

Why this illustrative book format?
Seeing is believing - Visuals inside are factual, hence precious and rare.

What does it contain?
It contains real-life images/sketches of the state of prison management and prison reforms we introduced, followed by the birth and growth of India Vision Foundation in Delhi Tihar Prisons from 1993 and beyond. Establishing the collaborative power of
Prevention- Correction-Rehabilitation

What is its message?
Reformation is possible, provided the proper management practices are adhered to with missionary zeal.
The objective is to "SAVE THE NEXT VICTIM"

Where are the contents sourced from?
The book "It's Always Possible" and the documentation from the India Vision Foundation

Who will benefit the most?
Society as a whole.

Yours truly

KIRAN BEDI
Inspector General Tihar Prisons, Delhi
1993-1995

TABLE OF CONTENTS

PREFACE

As a police officer, I sent many lawbreakers to prison to safeguard society from their criminal actions.

I noticed that many inmates released from jail were angry and revengeful.

The prison system was a contaminating institution, resembling a revolving door.

But what was causing this cycle?
I witnessed first-hand the prevailing 'inhuman' practices, which were leading to an increase in violence and gangsterism.

Upon their release, inmates were hostile and vindictive against society.

We, as a team comprising Dr. Jayadev Sarangi, K.R Kishore, P.R.Meena, Tarsem Kumar, D.P. Diwedi, Sunil Gupta and others resolved to grapple with the challenge head-on by creatively using existing resources.

This effort received international acclaim, including the Ramon Magsaysay Award 1994

This illustrative compilation is evidence of that transformation.

There were two options.

The first option was to let the status quo be and take the easy way out. Be reactive and punitive. The other was to be transformative and preventive.

It meant a comprehensive shift in how the institution was being administered - most of all in the mindsets of the supervisors.

There was no time to lose. It needed urgent surgery in the methodology of its leadership.

Prison management in India has never been the same since then.

SECTION- 1
WHAT I SAW

The Legacy

Tihar, one of India's most prominent high-security prisons, started in 1956 and was initially run by the State of Punjab. In 1966, the administration was transferred to the national capital of Delhi. This jail is known to house the most notorious of prisoners- terrorists, rapists, gangsters, and smugglers all mixed up in wards and contaminating each other.

Corruption was rampant, internal violence was widespread, and we even heard of women being maltreated!

The prison has a capacity of 2000 but houses 10,000 inmates

The Prevailing Vulture Culture

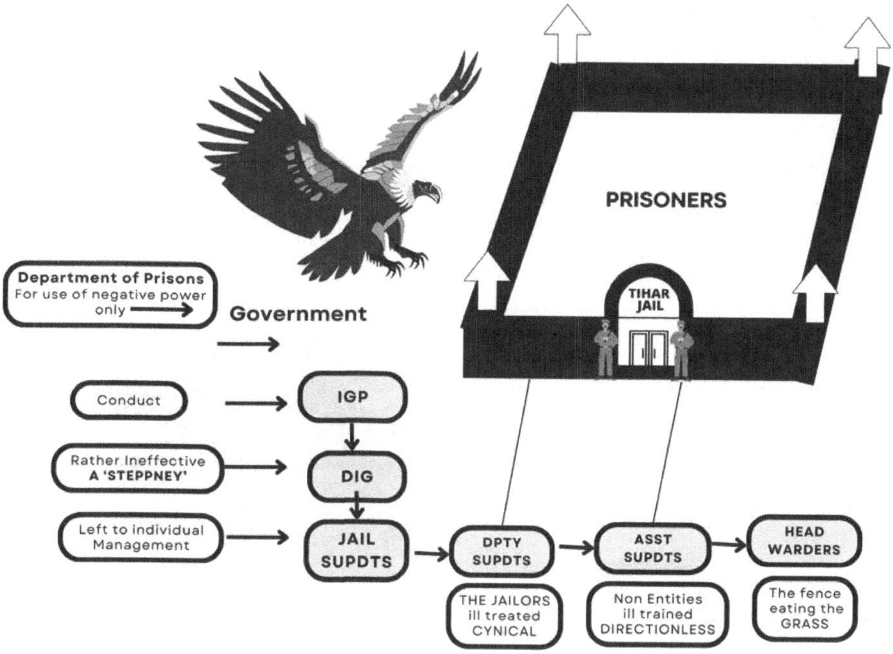

In May 1993, I was posted as Inspector General of Tihar Jail.What I saw was that there were problems of enormous magnitude. Ten thousand prisoners are waiting to be transformed, and the prison management was in a mess. The supervisory ranks were distant, the official hierarchy only existed to take punitive actions, and the culture that existed in the prison administration was akin to a vulture culture.

No Difference Between Night & Day

One night, I went on a round to see what Tihar was like at night. I was concerned and wanted to know if the prisoners slept well at night. But I was appalled to hear prisoners howling like animals. When I asked my SI what these noises were all about, he said, "Madam, they are all addicted to drugs, some taking an overdose of campose, some taking cough syrup, and others getting drugs from outside so sleep eludes them. Day and night were the same for them.

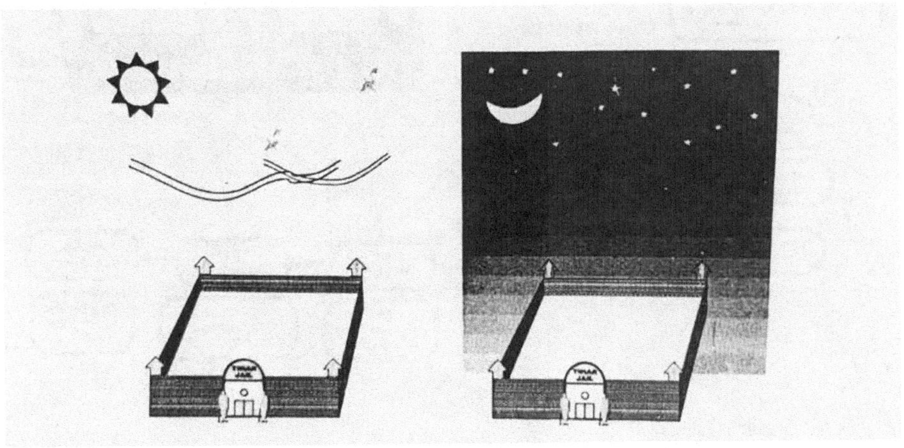

We had started with a system of 'head counts' and 'lock-ups'. It was a place where occupants did not sleep at night for various reasons. The night sounds resembled those of a zoo. A place inhabited by humans to whom it hardly mattered whether it was a day or night! This is how I felt when I first saw Tihar...

First Day At Office - A Punishment Posting

FIRST DAY IN OFFICE : ILLUSTRATED BY AN INMATE

On my first day at Tihar, I found little mice running over my feet as I sat on my office chair. It was said this was their home, as no occupant had been in this office long — a flurry of bird feathers scattered everywhere when I stood to turn on my desert cooler. It turned out that the cooler had not been operated for an extended period, and it housed a bird's nest.

Seeing that the rusted iron buckets in which the staff delivered the meals doubled up as mopping buckets and were used for washing clothes and storing water was appalling. As a result, the food had insects and flies, and the supplied dal was also highly diluted.

Prison Food as Depicted by an Inmate

Unhygienic and Unsanitary Food

Pilferages, Contamination Fights and Vandalism

Milk Pilferage

As I went about scrutinizing the jail over the next few weeks, I was both agonized and angered at the deplorable conditions in which the prisoners were living. They did not have access to proper basic facilities like hygienic food and water. The milk supplied had equal water and was not boiled before supplying to prisoners. The staff also pilfered, sold and shared among themselves. Tea was almost black and bitter.

During my rounds to the women's ward, one woman, agonised by the conditions there, poured her heart out to me and told me that once the rice that was served contained pieces of rusted wire, She somehow got the warder to call the duty officer and report it.

Iron in Rice

Insensitive Staff

Staff Vandalism

When women required fuel for cooking, dried prison chapatis became their preferred choice. They utilized these chapatis as a fuel source for preparing meals and brewing tea for themselves, the staff, and doctors. During the winter months, when the demand for tea increased, the chapatis were sold for 10 paise each. In instances when chapatis were unavailable, books were quickly taken and repurposed. It illustrates the kind of staff vandalism that occurred within the prison walls.

Water was the most precious item inside the prison, and there was no guarantee of it. There were very few hand pumps as opposed to the number of prisoners, and at times, one had to pump at least 50 times for water to come in the pumps. Although boards were saying the water was not potable, illiterate prisoners were seen gulping this water, Because of the water shortage, many women even cut their hair short.

Fighting over Water

Frequent fights would often break out at the handpump.

Children who accompanied their mothers, as permitted by Indian law until the age of six., lacked access to medical care, education and proper nutrition. They imitated and repeated whatever they heard the inmates speak.

Shocking Conversations by Children

Lack of Medical Services

Tuberculosis was rampant inside the prison. Prisoners pilfered cough syrups and sedatives. There was no drug abuse treatment program. After 2 PM, for all 10,000 prisoners, there was only 1 Doctor. Children had no medical cards and they suffered the most.

Gangsters Ruled The Roost

Visits

Corruption during family visits (mulaquat) was rampant.

Extent of Exploitation

White Water

Women a neglected species

SECTION- 2

WHAT WE DID

Creche Setup Inside

We carved out a separate space for children from the women's ward to have a space to play among themselves. Later we expanded

In India, the law permits incarcerated women to keep their children with them in prison until the age of six.

Monica Dhawan, Director India Vision Foundation Visiting The Creche at Tihar

We started a daycare centre catering to these children's holistic development through education, nutrition and proper healthcare.

Play Way Creche for Children Expanded with The Help of NGOs

Mobile Creches training women inmates as creche workers

Literacy for All Prisoners

Removing Illiteracy Among Women and Men

We began by correcting the biological clocks of the prisoners by adding day and evening activities, beginning with learning for all 10,000 prisoners. We took the help of schools from the city, asking them to donate used school books for all classes. Literate and skilled prisoners became educators.

Vocational Skills for Women

Vocational Training Towards Self-Reliance

Apart from regular education, we also focused on vocational training for prisoners. We tried to make headway into vocational training for the prisoners to keep them occupied even in their free time. We started teaching them book binding, file cover making, agarbatti incense stick rolling, chalk making, tailoring, TV and radio repair and computer training.

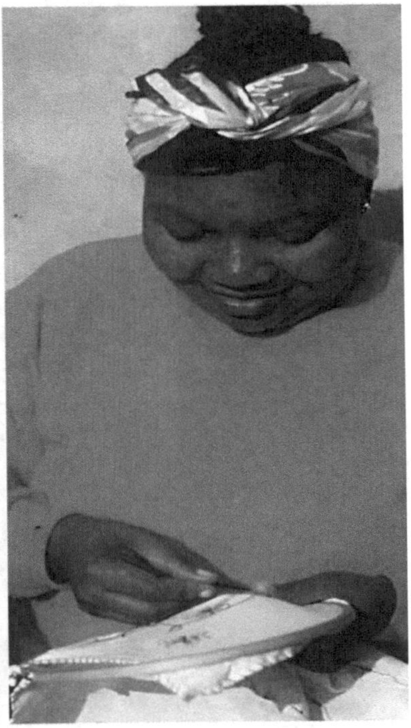

Women Inmates in Creative Sessions

Converting Garbage into Manure

Walking around the prison amidst the stench of garbage made me realize the need to clean up and recycle this. Excel Industries trained the staff and inmates to convert horticulture and vegetable waste into manure. The money generated became a welfare fund. We also collaborated with organizations like Sulabh International to extract biogas from the garbage before turning it into manure.

Turning Garbage into Manure

Tihar Bakery

We started a Bakery to provide fresh Bread and Confectionery to over 10,000 inmates.

Income Generated Went to Prisoners Welfare Fund

The Petition Box

To contain corruption and be preventive, I started the mobile petition box system so prisoners could write and share their problems and other developments. We started this on 1st June 1993, exactly a month after I took over as IG prisons in May 1993.

The locked mobile petition box was a simple system of grievance redressal. It was a wooden box, painted green, with the number of prisoners written on it. Each prison was given a different box, and four constables/clerks were earmarked by rotation to take these boxes to the jails. The keys of the petition boxes remained with me, and every evening, I would open the boxes, read the letters and plan what needed to be done with a sense of urgency regarding the issues brought to my notice in confidence.

Feedback System - The Petition Box

Community & Harmony

We brought much community harmony within the prison by celebrating festivals of all faiths. All such special events were celebrated together, and prisoners cooked, served, shared and cared for each other.

A photograph of one such event

Spirituality

During my visit to the women's ward, I inquired, "Do you read? Do you practice yoga?" The response was a resounding 'No', as they lacked the facilities for both activities. Then I asked, "Would you like to read and do yoga?" they chorused a joyful 'Yes.

'This moment marked the inception of spiritual programs in Tihar Jail.

Regular Meditation Sessions

Vipasanna (Meditation)

The magical metamorphosis happened when an Assistant Superintendent told me about Vipassana, a form of meditation known to help prisoners. We immediately connected with Mr Ram Singh and requested that Vipassana meditation be started in the prison. We were blessed to have Goenkaji and Mataji stay in jail for 10 days to teach this meditation to 1000 prisoners for the first time. This led to the inauguration of a permanent Vipassana prison centre to continue with the courses.

Men and Women in Meditation course

History Made

Over 1000 inmates sat in the Vipassana Meditation course. The largest ever conducted inside any prison in the world.

TESTIMONIALS ON VIPASSANA

A Norwegian Prisoner - 1

THE EXPERIENCE OF VIPASSANA IN TIHAR

As I went through my first Vipassana ten-day course I realized that as long there is going to be pleasures in life there will also have to be pain. Learning how to handle my pain just through sitting, for ten days was my most difficult experience ever. Vipassana thought me how to smile when I'm sad and how to be happy without becoming hysterical.

Vipassana is cre[illegible]tive. Seing things as they really are. That all phenomena are epheral, and there is of no use clinging or craving towards them. Better just to aucsept the external world as it is learning how to see with eyes of wisdom from a

A Norwegian Prisoner - 2

internal viewpoint. Just observing one's physical sensations and mind realizing how it's all connected. How every action has a direct effect, Karma, and learning to act instead of merely reacting.

That it is possible to be sitting for theese courses while serving time in jail is very beneficial. Not only for the individual meditators but also for society as a whole. Time for reflection and meditation should be obligatory in every Jail as it gives the word reform a new meaning. To me Vipassana is a tool of reforming myself, improving my ways of life. It's the real thing as it doesn't mix religion or sectarian rituals whith the art of meditation. It is simply a scientific instruction on how to live in the present, more aware, and more awake to see reality, as it is.

It is my deep wish and I hope from my heart that as many as possible will benefit from the precious teachings of the Bhudda, the enlightened one, the dhamma and the Sangha the community which now even

A Norwegian Prisoner - 3

arases inside jail. May the flower of dhamma grow bigger and higher in order to benifit all beings. May all be happy!

Yours faithfully

Leo Sande Gasnier
Convict

Vipassnna Center Inaugurated at Tihar

Tihar Over Booked

Soon, the community and the media entered the prison to help us improve the situation. The press was given limited access to cover the prison reforms without much glorification. International media like BBC, New Times, CNN, and others connected with us to learn about our work and to give us visibility. Students, too, were allowed inside to intern or do research

The most happening place in town? Tihar Jail, of course !

Continuity in emergence... Courtesy : The Times of India, April 9, 1998. Caricaature by Neelab

9th April 1998 Times of India

Emergence of 3C Model

We transformed the legacy of a notorious prison, characterized by crime, corruption, and violence that we inherited into a 3 C model of Collective, Corrective, and Community based policing, which has been embraced by prisons worldwide.

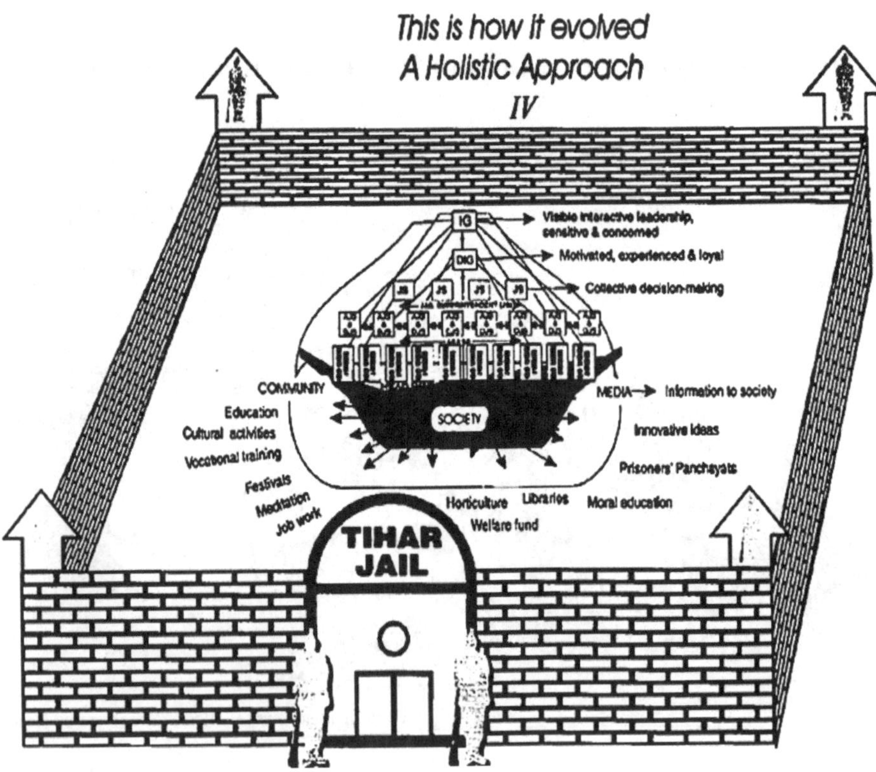

SECTION- 3

BIRTH OF INDIA VISION FOUNDATION

BIRTH OF INDIA VISION FOUNDATION

India Vision®
Foundation
#SaveTheNextVictim™

Acceptance of Ramon Magsaysay Award

The award has propelled me to consolidate and expand my work. For this, I have registered with a trust called India Vision. I am breathing life into it at this moment. It will carry forward projects in prison reform, drug abuse prevention, women empowerment, mental disability, and sports promotion. I would appreciate your help in these projects. I accept the Ramon Magsaysay Award with total gratitude to the Foundation and the Philippines on behalf of my team, comprising Police-Prison-People and my family from India.

Manila, Philippines, 31st August 1994

– 6 SEP 1994

Bedi to launch prison reform foundation

Press Trust of India

NEW DELHI, September 5

Mrs Kiran Bedi, inspector general of Tihar jail, today announced launching of a foundation to carry forward projects in the field of prison reform, drug abuse prevention, empowerment of women, mental disability and sports promotion.

Mrs Bedi, who returned yesterday after receiving the Ramon Magsaysay award for public service for 1994, told newsmen that the 50,000 US dollars (approximately Rs 15 lakhs) from the award would form the main corpus for the "Indian Vision Foundation."

Besides, the Filipino-Indian chamber of commerce has also joined the foundation for collaborative projects and pledged a donation of $ 10,000 and their president will be a member of the board of trustees, Mrs Bedi said.

Stating that the award had propelled her to consolidate and expand her work, Mrs Bedi, who brought a series of reforms in the...

Institutionalization of the Foundation

What is India Vision Foundation & Why?

It works to save the next victim. It means that if an inmate leaves the prison with anger and revenge, they look for their next victim and continue the cycle of crime, victim, jail, bail, victim, and back to prison. The prison system is both for deterrence and reform. It fails in its ultimate purpose if it does not address the latter.

What does it do? Who all do we serve?

It works with men, women and children who have come with their mothers inside the prison.

How does it work?

It works on education, skill, and ethical reformation. It also trains the prison personnel through in-person and online programs.

Where does it serve?

It works with prisons around the country and provides an internationally recognized model for prison reforms

The Uniqueness of this Program

It is a unique program as it works with children of Incarcerated parents inside and outside the prisons, focusing on need-based nurturance and interventions.

Looking ahead

The route to crime prevention is reform and reintegration of all who undergo imprisonment. Many need-based programs can be practised. This section of the book is to help spur actions that can work in different settings. It is based on the philosophy that we save the next victim by providing nurturance to the children of prisoners and those released.

4s Model

INSIDE PRISON PROGRAM : READINESS TO RELEASE

This 4S model aims to reform inmates (men, women and children). It focuses on S- Shiksha or Education, S-Sanskaar- Values, S-Swasth-Health care and S-Skills.

All these four pillars prepare the inmates to lead a respectful life of reintegration post-release.

SHIKSHA

SANSKAR

SHIKSHA

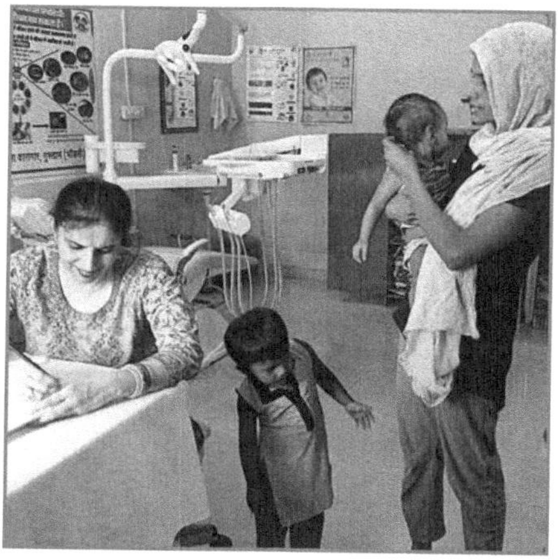

SANSKAR

2006 Hon'ble Supreme Court Judgement

The Hon'ble Justice Upadhyay's judgment observed that women prisoners' rights differ from those of the general prison population.

Hence, special provisions for women prisoners and their children should be made inside the prisons.

Children of Vulnerable Families

The Children of Vulnerable Families (CVF) Program aims to mainstream and educate the children of incarcerated families after the age of 6 years, ensuring their all-round well-being and development through continuous education and psychosocial support.

The goal is to help them achieve their academic, social, and emotional aspirations and save them from becoming a victim of their Parental Incarceration.

Students with Dr Kiran Bedi

Training of Prisoners

Tailoring

Haircutting

Fateh

(Triumph Over Tragedy)

A book handwritten by the beneficiaries.

Fateh is a compilation of real-life accounts of children of parents who went to prison. They battled extreme circumstances and came out victors. The stories have been collected in the original handwriting of the children.

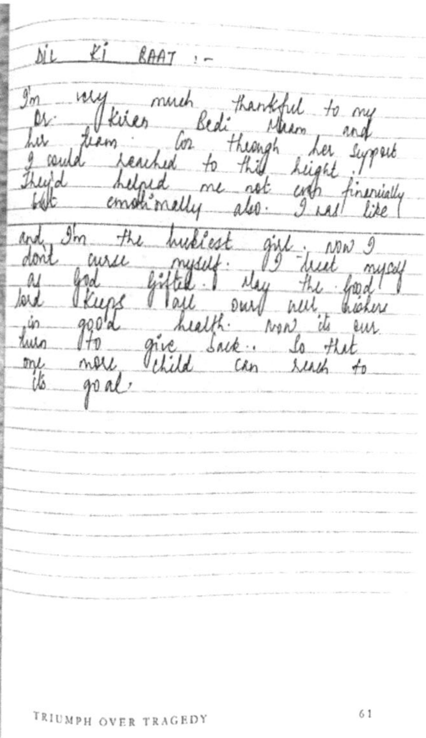

DIL KI BAAT :-

I'm very much thankful to my Dr. Kiran Bedi Mam and her team. Cos through her support I could reached to this height. They'd helped me not only financially but emotionally also. I was like [illegible]

and I'm the luckiest girl. now I don't curse myself. I treat myself as God gifted. May the good lord keeps all our well wishers in good health. now its our turn to give back.. so that one more child can reach to its goal.

TRIUMPH OVER TRAGEDY 61

Radio Parvaaz

The Prison Community Radio
By
India Vision Foundation

Providing a voice to those incarcerated

Training of Prison Officials

Person

Online

UNODC

Strengthening Prison
of Interactive

United Nations
Office on Drugs and Crime
India Vision Foundation
Unlocking Health Behind Bars:
Strengthening Prison Healthcare and Launch
of Interactive Prison Toolkit

Footprints

13,14,672 TOTAL REACH OF THE FOUNDATION

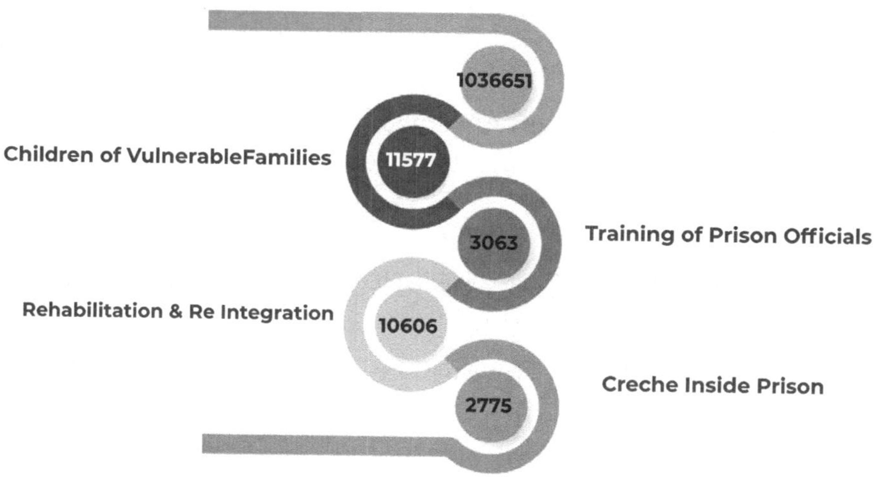

172 Prisons

14 States

02 Union Territories

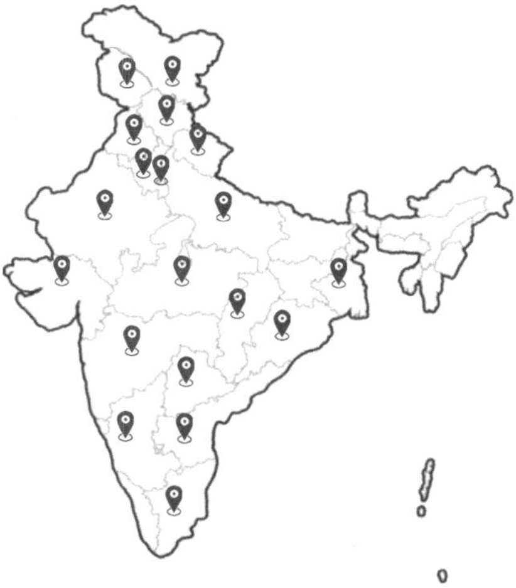

Research Studies

2011-12

- Once there was a girl born in jail..." - A narrative study of a group of children of incarcerated parents in India by Hanna Johansson in the Autumn of 2011
- Glimpses Of 'Exploring Childhood In Tihar by CECED (Centre for Early Childhood and Education) in 2012

2013-14

- Impact study of 'Children of Vulnerable Families' project of the India Vision Foundation by Soceo Consulting Services Private Limited, Kolkata

2018-19

- AN IMPACT ASSESSMENT OF THE DHUN PROJECT: A Qualitative & Quantitative Study by Protiviti India
- Impact of 'YOGA TEACHER TRAINING PROGRAM' (YTTP) by India Vision Foundation
- An Analysis of the Impact of IVF's Reformation Program in Prisons through the Experiences and Satisfaction of its Beneficiaries and Prison Staff's by India Vision Foundation
- Impact Assessment Study: Remedial Education Programme for Children of Incarcerated Parents by the Learning & Development Vertical, India Vision Foundation

2019-20

- IMPACT OF COVID-19 ON INSIDE PRISON INMATES By Protiviti India in September 2020
- IMPACT OF COVID-19 ON RELEASED INMATES - I Situational & Need Analysis Study By Protiviti India in September 2020
- IMPACT OF COVID-19 ON CHILDREN OF PRISONERS By Protiviti India in September 2020

- Effects of COVID-19 on Children of Prison Inmates: A Rapid Survey Study Analysis by Giulia Guccione

2020-21

- Karma Centre for Counselling & Wellbeing: Need of Mental Health Intervention for Male Inmates, Mostly Undertrials Between the Ages of 18-21 Years, of District Prison of Gurugram, Haryana
- Smriti Sikri, M.Phil. Dissertation Titled "Experiences of Women in Conflict with Law During Their Legal Recourse in Delhi", DSSW under Prof. Neena Pandey
- IMPACT ASSESSMENT OF THE PROJECT NEW HORIZON By Protiviti India Member Private Limited
- Need Assessment Survey to Understand the Holistic Needs of the Children of Incarcerated Fathers of Dasna Prison, Ghaziabad Inmates by Department of Psychology, CHRIST (Deemed to be University), Delhi NCR

2021-22

- Parul Soni, Master's in Development from Azim Premji University, Bangalore: "Exploring the Health Conditions of Women Ex-Undertrial Prisoners in the Delhi NCR Region"
- Siri Reddy (UCL Scholar) University College London, UK: Study on the Rehabilitative Experiences of Ex-Prisoners in India: The Push for a Central Prison Reform Program

2022-23

- Department of Psychology, IILM University Gurgram: "Studying the Impact of the Interventions (Khushali Project & Project Sabrang) Provided to the Inmates of Gurugram Jail"
- Study on the Invisible Victims of Maternal Incarceration by Pearly Sanil, Program Manager, CVF, Jamia Millia Islamia University, Delhi

- Impact of Social Support on the Young Adults of Incarcerated Mothers by Pearly Paul, PhD Study, Jamia Millia Islamia University, Delhi
- Girika Batra, MSc. Forensic Psychologist from National Forensic Science University, Gandhinagar Gujarat: The Effect of Rehabilitation Activities on the Psychological Well-Being of Female Prison Inmates
- Izeen Fatima (Psychology Graduate, Jamia Millia Islamia University): Impact of Dance Movement Therapy on Male Prison Inmates
- Palak Gujarathi (MSc. Forensic Psychologist from National Forensic Science University, Gandhinagar Gujarat): Impact Study on the Role of India Vision Foundation in Empowering Children in High-Risk Environments
- Baseline Study in Loni Community: India Vision Foundation Team & Apabrita Das Adhikari, MSc. Forensic Psychology, National Forensic Science University Gandhinagar Gujarat

2020-21

- Report on Prison Nurseries by Stuti Shah, Doctoral Scholar, Columbia University, US
- Training Program Impact Study by Poulomi, Jindal School of Behavioural Sciences, OP Jindal University, Haryana
- Impact Study by GL Bajaj Institute of Management and Research, Greater Noida, UP
- Work-Family Conflict and Job Satisfaction among the Correctional Officers of India by Preetika Kedia, Jindal School of Behavioral Sciences, OP Jindal University, Haryana
- Beyond Carcerality and Invisibilisation: Exploring Work Lives of the Incarcerated Persons by Nikita Garg, MA in Labour Studies and Practice, Tata Institute of Social Sciences
- Poster Analysis by Prof. Iryna, Jindal University and Ms Anushri Shevde, Psychologist, CHRIST University, Ghaziabad, UP

Milestones

1994-2004

- India Vison Foundation is Born : Dr Kiran Bedi receives Ramon Magsaysay Award
- Our Journey Begins in Tihar: Inside Prison & Crèche Program launched
- Children of Vulnerable Families Program launched

2005-2015

- Operating Model : 3S model of reformation
- Fateh Book was published
- 1st Outreach Program Launched : of Reeta Peshawaria Fellowship Award

- 1st Community Center for Children
- Launch of Training of Prison Officials and Rehabilitation & Reintegration program

2016 - 2024

- 25 years of service completed
- Outreach program : Demonstrative Learning intervention was launched
- 3S to 4S model of reformation

- Launch of Flagship Therapy Modules
- Transit from Residential School to Family Support Model
- Experiential Learning launched

- Prison Community Radio wins the prestigious New York Music Festival Award
- **1 million lives** impacted & presence across **100 +** Prison locations

Awards and Appreciation

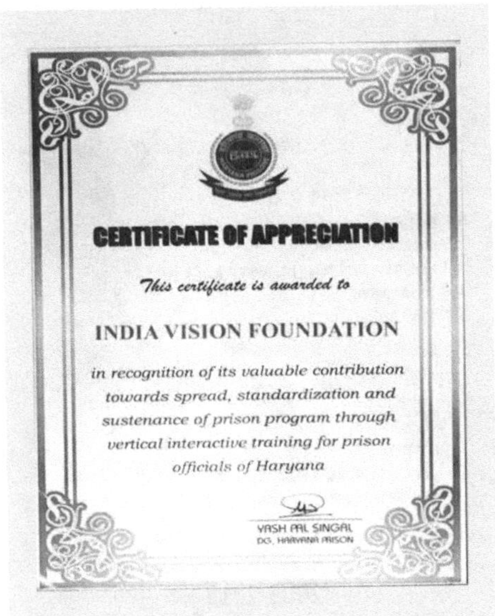

CERTIFICATE OF APPRECIATION

This certificate is awarded to

INDIA VISION FOUNDATION

in recognition of its valuable contribution towards spread, standardization and sustenance of prison program through vertical interactive training for prison officials of Haryana

YASH PAL SINGAL
DG, HARYANA PRISON

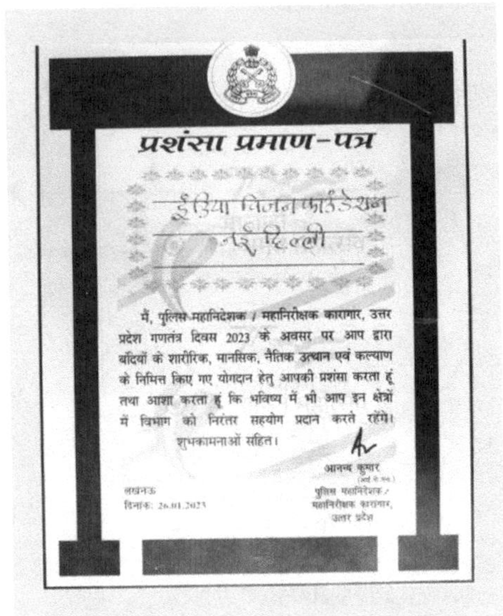

प्रशंसा प्रमाण-पत्र

इंडिया विजन फाउंडेशन
नई दिल्ली

मैं, पुलिस महानिदेशक / महानिरीक्षक कारागार, उत्तर प्रदेश गणतंत्र दिवस 2023 के अवसर पर आप द्वारा बंदियों के शारीरिक, मानसिक, नैतिक उत्थान एवं कल्याण के निमित्त किए गए योगदान हेतु आपकी प्रशंसा करता हूं तथा आशा करता हूं कि भविष्य में भी आप इन क्षेत्रों में विभाग को निरंतर सहयोग प्रदान करते रहेंगे।

शुभकामनाओं सहित।

आनन्द कुमार
पुलिस महानिदेशक / महानिरीक्षक कारागार, उत्तर प्रदेश

लखनऊ
दिनांक: 26.01.2023

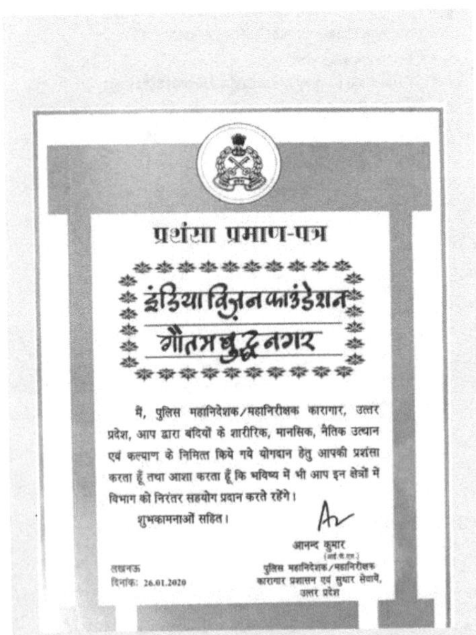

प्रशंसा प्रमाण-पत्र

इंडिया विज़न फाउंडेशन
गौतमबुद्धनगर

मैं, पुलिस महानिदेशक/महानिरीक्षक कारागार, उत्तर प्रदेश, आप द्वारा बंदियों के शारीरिक, मानसिक, नैतिक उत्थान एवं कल्याण के निमित्त किये गये योगदान हेतु आपकी प्रशंसा करता हूँ तथा आशा करता हूँ कि भविष्य में भी आप इन क्षेत्रों में विभाग को निरंतर सहयोग प्रदान करते रहेंगे।

शुभकामनाओं सहित।

आनन्द कुमार
पुलिस महानिदेशक/महानिरीक्षक कारागार प्रशासन एवं सुधार सेवायें, उत्तर प्रदेश

लखनऊ
दिनांक: 26.01.2020

YES FOUNDATION

YES! I am the CHANGE

GRANT & ACCELERATOR 2018

India Vision Foundation

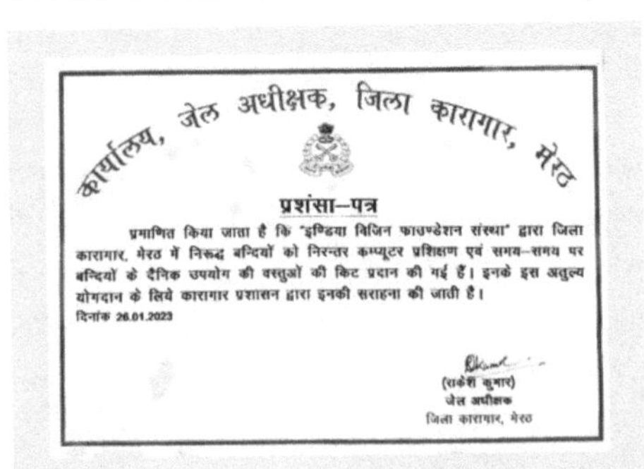

कार्यालय, जेल अधीक्षक, जिला कारागार, मेरठ

प्रशंसा–पत्र

प्रमाणित किया जाता है कि "इण्डिया विजिन फाउण्डेशन संस्था" द्वारा जिला कारागार, मेरठ में निरुद्ध बन्दियों को निरन्तर कम्प्यूटर प्रशिक्षण एवं समय–समय पर बन्दियों के दैनिक उपयोग की वस्तुओं की किट प्रदान की गई हैं। इनके इस अतुल्य योगदान के लिये कारागार प्रशासन द्वारा इनकी सराहना की जाती है।

दिनांक 26.01.2023

(राकेश कुमार)
जेल अधीक्षक
जिला कारागार, मेरठ

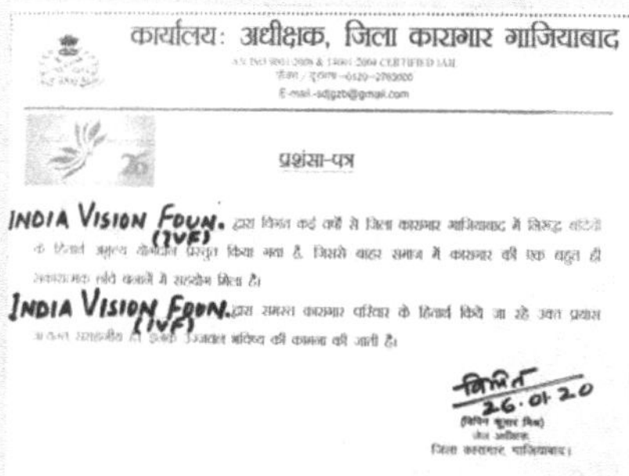
कार्यालय: अधीक्षक, जिला कारागार गाजियाबाद
E-mail-sdjgzb@gmail.com
प्रशंसा-पत्र
INDIA VISION FOUN. (IVF)
INDIA VISION FOUN. (IVF)
26.01.20

NEWYORKFESTIVALS
RADIO AWARDS
2022 FINALIST DIPLOMA
India Vision Foundation
RADIO PARVAAZ
"SHAME TO FAME - A Reformation story"
HEROES

Certificate of Excellence
INDIA VISION FOUNDATION

SILVER - SDG 8
India Vision Foundation
Global Sustainability Awards 2024

Golden Mic Award
2024

americares
Abbott
SPIRIT OF HUMANITY
8TH ANNUAL AWARDS
Certificate
of REGIONAL WINNER
awarded to
India Vision Foundation
for contribution in the field of
CHILD CARE
September 14, 2017, Mumbai
Distinguished Jury

Health

MAHATMA AWARD
महात्मा पुरस्कार
AMIT SACHDEVA INITIATIVE
Mahatma Award for Social Good and Impact
presented to
India Vision Foundation
INDIA | USA | UK | SOUTH AFRICA
www.mahatmaaward.com

India Vision Foundation
INDIA VISION FOUNDATION

And the journey continues.....

Team India Vision Foundation

Celebrating New Year 3rd January, 2025

Team India Vision Foundation and Beneficiaries 2024

Gratitude

Director General of Prisons Additional Director General of Prisons Inspector General of Prisons, Deputy Inspector General of Prisons Superintendents & all other Prison Officials

Name of the Prison Department

- Bihar Department of Prisons and Correctional Services Chhattisgarh Jail Department
- Department of Prisons and Correctional Administration, UT, Chandigarh
- Delhi Prison Administration
- Prisons Department of the Government of Haryana
- Department of Prisons and Correctional Services, Himachal Pradesh Jammu & Kashmir Prisons Department
- Department of Home, Jail, and Disaster Management Jharkhand
- Jails and Correctional Services (JCS) Department of Madhya Pradesh
- Maharashtra Prison Department
- Department of Prisons and Correctional Services, Government of Meghalaya
- Directorate of Prisons, Nagaland
- Odisha, Directorate of Prisons and Correctional Services
- Punjab Prisons Department.
- Rajasthan Prisons Department
- Prisons Administration & Reform Services, Uttar Pradesh
- Department of Prison, Government of Uttarakhand.
- Department of Correctional Administration, West Bengal

Ajay Goyal for all the photographs Edited by Grammarly

Saji Nair of Intime Reprographics, New Delhi for the Design Layouts

Gratitude to all who made this transformation possible

The Book Team
From India Vision Foundation

Dr. Amrita Bahl

Dhairya Kumar

Ghazal Khan

Monica Dhawan

Renu Nag

Rinkey Kumari

Shakira Scolt

Shivani Arora

Sumitra Rai

Blessings

S.N Goenka ji and Mata ji conducted the Vipassana course for 1000 inmates

Illustrations and selected content have been sourced from the book